How to Unlock Your Full Potential

WORKBOOK

Eleven keys to leader Success

Frederick Cross * Dr. Amanda Goodson * Odetta Scott

AMANDA GOODSON
Goodson Leadership Workbook™

ISBN- 13:978-0615922348
ISBN- 10:0615922341

Printed in the U.S.A.

First Edition

How to Unlock Your Full Potential

WORKBOOK

Keys to leader Success

Frederick Cross * Dr. Amanda Goodson * Odetta Scott

AMANDA GOODSON
Goodson Leadership Workbook™

Table of Contents

Acknowledgements

We dedicate this book to our leadership partners, families and friends. Thank you for supporting our desire to transform leaders and encourage others to unleash their power to successfully achieve their full potential!

Introduction

This workbook is written to enhance our original book, *"Unlock Your Full Potential –Keys to Leader Success"*. This workbook is for those who want a deep, hands-on approach to reaching their full potential in creative ways that are proven and can be documented.

Let's begin on a deeper journey to unlock your full potential and influence others around you in a more powerful way. This interactive workbook is written to engage with the reader to achieve peak states and levels of performance on a routine basis. This creative tool will answer pressing leadership questions with the future state in mind.

As stated in our book: Most people possess the power to make things happen in a way that will transform their organization, situation, or community in an awesome way. Unlocking your full potential is an essential part of getting what you want in life. This book contains several keys that will unlock your full potential and ensure your success as an outstanding leader.

People who utilize the keys highlighted in this book will see remarkable improvement in their relationships and in their performance at all levels. As a direct result, they will be able to affect positive outcomes and make things happen around them. Those who act on what they know will develop the skills necessary to reach peak states within the organizations they influence.

We believe every individual has been granted the ability to accomplish great things. Greatness has many facets and levels. Greatness carries power; and the power to complete our tasks can be done well with the right desire.

Based on our mini-book, the information in this workbook, *How to Unlock Your Full Potential,* will serve to equip you with the tools that will provide valuable insights into how to lead with power and influence. People who unlock their full potential have the ability to lead more effectively by transforming themselves and others around them. A leader's ability to be authentic, achieve goals that have been set, continue on a path to pursue professional growth, and influence others in amazing ways all speak to the leader's competency.

This workbook is meant to arouse your thinking and cause you to be more creative, enhance your leadership knowledge, and develop a style that will impact others around you with power. As you write on these pages, keep an open mind so that you will be able to see how unlocking your full potential affects you, learn new skills to transform your thinking, and to touch those whose lives you influence.

Enjoy the exercises written in this workbook and use this resource as a guide so that you will continue to reach your full potential!

CHAPTER 1

Effective Leadership

Leaders Lead!

F.E. Cross

1. Effective Leadership

What is Effective Leadership?

Effective Leadership is the ability to guide, direct or influence people, groups, and/or teams to achieve stated goals.

Why is it important?

Achieving goals lies at the core of organizational success.

What does effective leadership look like?

Teams achieving stated goals in a seamless manner.

Listed below are several effective leadership traits:
1. Be committed
2. Know the traits that the group values in a leader
3. Develop a solid vision and goals
4. Effective communication – communicate-communicate-communicate
5. Develop situational leadership – a leadership style that is most effective to help the team achieve its goals

Do you agree? Disagree? Let's determine what you think are effective leadership traits in the exercises below.

Effective Leadership Exercise #1
List four (4) effective leaders that you admire:
1.
2.
3.
4.

Document the top three (3) traits that made each effective leader listed above successful.
1.
2.
3.

Do a comparison of traits that made each of the successful leaders successful. Look for and document the common characteristics of the successful leaders:
1.
2.
3.

Effective Leadership Exercise #2

List four (4) leaders that were not effective: *(Note: You can learn just as much about leadership from an ineffective leader as you can from an effective leader)*

1.
2.
3.
4.

Document the top three (3) threats that made each leader listed above ineffective:

1.
2.
3.

Do a comparison of traits that made each of the ineffective leaders less than effective. Look for and document the common characteristics of each of these leaders:

1.
2.
3.

Effective Leadership Exercise #3

Compile a list to the top five (5) traits that you want to demonstrate as a leader:

1.
2.
3.
4.
5.

Compile a list to the top five (5) traits that you do not want to demonstrate as a leader:

1.
2.
3.
4.
5.

Congratulations. You now have your leadership / relationship "Top 10". Commit to demonstrate the "Do's" into every aspect of life and to eliminate the "Don'ts" from your life.

CHAPTER 2

Transform

The ability to transform into the leader you are purposed to be is inside of you.
It is waiting to emerge!

Dr. Amanda Goodson

2. Transform

What is Leader Transformation?

Transformation is the process of understanding a new way of seeing you. Transformation is the process of becoming the inherently excellent, brilliant and illumined leader you are purposed to be. It is going from who you are now to a place of becoming who you are purposed to be. It is like becoming a lead butterfly.

Why is it important?

It is important because leaders lead others to a place of purpose. Others will look to you to find their place in the organization. By example, you will show them how to change their lives toward the direction of what they are created to become.

The team will do a better job when they transform.

How do I understand how to become a transformed leader?

1. It is like a caterpillar turning into a butterfly. The caterpillar has everything it needs inside of it to become a butterfly.

2. Study the caterpillar.   Study the butterfly. Notice the differences between the two. Use that analogy to make changes in your unlimited potential as a leader.

3. Over the process of time, and with the right environment, the change happens.

4. We should seek that place by viewing our leadership as relevant, needed and powerful.

5. As we seek to lead well, change our perspective on life and recognize our potential contributions to the organization, transformation will begin.

6. We should identify what may need to change in our lives that would be a greater benefit to the organization and to unlock our potential.

Transformation Exercise #1

1. Take a rubber band and hold it between your thumb and index finger in both hands.

2. Stretch it out vertically. (It should create tension between the two points)

3. The bottom of the rubber band represents where you are now.

4. The top of the rubber band represents where you are purposed to be.

5. The distance between the two points is the creative tension, or unlocked potential, that needs to be released.

6. Bring your fingers together and release the tension.

7. As you move closer to the new place of change, you will experience less tension.

Transformation Exercise #2

In the space below document your answers to the following questions:

How would I define my leadership style right now?
1.
2.
3.
4.
5.

What do I do well as a leader?
1.
2.
3.
4.
5.

What do I need to improve in my life as a leader?
1.
2.
3.
4.
5.

As a leader, in what areas do I need significant change?
1.
2.
3.
4.
5.

In lists 3 and 4 (last two questions), which answers are the same?
1.
2.
3.
4.
5.

Transformation Exercise #3

In the space below, write a plan of action of how you will change the areas identified in the previous section:

Consider the following:

- *Training or classes you could take*
- *Coaching from a recognized expert in the field*
- *Spending more time focused on the improvement*
- *Get a trusted accountability partner to help you throughout the process*

My transformation plan includes:

_____

_____

_____

From this day forward, I will take the following actions to improve and unlock my leadership potential.

_____

_____

_____

CHAPTER 3

Authenticity

Authenticity is the alignment of head, mouth, heart, and feet - thinking, saying, feeling, and doing the same thing - consistently. This builds trust; and followers love leaders they can trust.

Lance Secretan

3.   Authenticity

What is authenticity?

Authenticity is the choice a leader makes to show up, and to be real (be one's self) when they do show up.

Why is it important?

People have a desire to connect with and to follow leaders that can be themselves in situations. Whether that situation is good or bad – be real. Being authentic may require you as the leader to do some self-reflection about your behavior and leadership style in order to drive to closure on the tasks at hand. The exercises below will assist in this self-reflection.

How do I know if I am being authentic? Are you being true to yourself?

1.   How self-aware are you? You must be self-aware.

2.   You must know and understand your worth. You are talented and always bring something different to the table.

3.   You have to be clear on what your value system is and what you believe in. In the event that you are in a situation where your beliefs are challenged, you need to have enough self-awareness to be able to see it and to understand.

Authenticity Exercise #1

In the space below document your answers to the following questions:

Take a moment to reflect and list four (4) situations where you felt your behavior was less than acceptable.

1.

2.

3.

4.

For each situation – identify why you feel your behavior was less than acceptable?

1.

2.

3.

4.

What would you change or improve about your behavior if the same situation were to occur in the near future?

1.

2.

3.

4.

Can you identify any themes? List your themes below?

1.

2.

3.

4.

Develop and document a plan to improve each of the behaviors you would change above.

Theme 1:_____

Theme 2:_____

Theme 3:_____

Theme 4:_____

Authenticity Exercise #2
Refer back to the Effective Leadership exercises from Chapter 1 (ELT). You documented leaders you admired and their positive traits. With that in mind document your positive traits as a leader (MPT).

ELT

ELT

ELT

MPT

MPT

MPT

Also, capture the ineffective leader traits (ILT) and your non-positive traits (MIT) below.

ILT

ILT

ILT

MIT

MIT

MIT

Reflecting on what you have documented, determine which traits you want to START displaying; which traits you display you want to CONTINUE displaying; and which traits you want to STOP portraying. What do you need to adjust to become more self-aware?

CHAPTER 4

Achievement

Achievement -- the measure of success

F.E. Cross

4. Achievement

What is Leadership Achievement?
Leadership Achievement is the art and/or process of achieving goals.

Why is it important?
Achieving goals is core to organizational success.

What does achieving goals look like?
Achieving goals occurs when you successfully complete well-planned goals with and through others.

How do I understand how to become that achiever?

1.   Documenting goals (those things you want to successfully achieve) is the first step in evaluating your achievement level.

2.   As a youth, did you have any wildly insane goals? I did; I wanted to be an astronaut. I developed and implemented a plan.

3.   When I completed a goal, I celebrated. It is very important to give yourself credit and celebrate for things you achieve.

Leadership Achievement Exercise #1:
The first step to leadership achievement is to define it. As a leader, you define what achievement looks like for you. *(Note: Is it to be in the C Suite; is it to have a great family life; is it to make a lot of money? Whatever it is; you define it, and you make it happen.)*

Leadership Achievement Exercise #:2
Document the top five (5) most important things to you (i.e. Family, Career, Money, or Standing in the community); whatever you believe is most important to you. **Note: This is your deepest feeling and it is for your information only. Share it with others, only if you feel comfortable in doing so. Do not let anyone force you to share this if you do not want to.**
1.
2.
3.
4.
5.

Using the list from exercise #2 development and document your top three (3) goals:
1.
2.
3.

Using the goals you developed, document what you are willing to do to achieve those goals *(Note: These should be as specific as possible, and this list of "Willing To" could be one (1) thing or twenty (20); you make the decision):*
1.
2.
3.
4.
5.

Congratulations! You now have your goals; you know what your priorities are; and you know what you are willing to do to achieve those goals. Now, develop and document a vision statement for achieving those goals and a plan to achieve your vision(s). We have provided a template for career achievement. Please use is to help develop you career plan. Also use a similar process / plan to develop your other goals.

CHAPTER 5

Growth and Development

Without growth and development, even the greatest leaders' progression can be stunted. To be a dynamic leader, growth and development is essential!

Odetta Scott

5. Growth & Development

What is growth and development?

> Growth is the step of going from one phase to a further advanced phase in the same arena. Development is the process that gets you from one phase to the next.

Why is it important?

> As a leader, the notion is that you are striving to do things in excellence and to be a great performer and be an individual others desire to follow. As a leader, growth is required to get to the next level and perform better where you are. After every success, challenge yourself to be just as successful on the next more complex assignment. Identifying those areas where you need to improve in order to make an impact (development plan), often times require a plan. Growth and development go hand in hand in effective leadership.

How do I know if I am getting better at growth & development?

1. Growth and development is something that happens over a period of time and often takes several cycles of learning.

2. Reflect on a personal behavior that you would like to improve. You have told yourself many times that you needed to get better at this behavior (ex. Jumping to a conclusion without looking at all the data).

3. Since that time, how many instances have you actually taken a step back to evaluate all the data before jumping to a conclusion? If this answer is on the positive side, this shows growth & development.

Growth & Development Exercise #1
In the space below, document your answers to the following questions:
Based on your Leadership Achievement Goals (Chapter 4 Exercises), perform a SPOT analysis.
S – Strength is defined as the traits/characteristics that give you an advantage in reaching your goals (Internal, Positive)
1.
2.
3.

P – Potential Areas of Improvement are defined as the traits/characteristics where you can improve in reaching your goals (Internal, Negative)
1.
2.
3.

O – Opportunity is defined traits/characteristics/situations that you can exploit to your advantage (External, Positive)
1.
2.
3.

T – Threat is defined as elements in the environment that could create/pose as a barrier to you in attaining your goal (External, Negative)
1.
2.
3.

Growth & Development Exercise #2
Identify four (4) areas where you feel you are not performing as you should be (growth areas).
1.
2.
3.
4.

For each growth area, create a development plan to assist in improving your performance. Your development plan should not be limited to course work only. Consider what other types of engagements you need that would help you improve (mentor, experiential opportunities, etc.)

Growth Area 1:_____
1.
2.
3.
4.
5.

Growth Area 2:_____
1.
2.
3.
4.
5.

Growth Area 3:_____

1.

2.

3.

4.

5.

Growth Area 4:_____

1.

2.

3.

4.

5.

Congratulations; you now have a documented development plan to attack your areas of growth. Stick to your plan, and then watch your performance improve in those identified areas.

CHAPTER 6

Influence

The power stoked in influence is undeniable – gain a bit of that power, wield it wisely, and watch your world change!

Odetta Scott

6.   Influence

What is influence?

> Influence can be defined as an intangible or indirect power that can affect an individual or a course of events.

Why is it important?

> Leaders often get things done through others. To complete the task at hand, leaders must possess the ability to motivate people and sell their idea to drive the vision. Let's take a look at a few exercises to help you and gauge where you are in the area of influence.

How do I understand how to get better at using influence?

1.   Realize that regardless of your title, you have the ability to leverage influence and drive change within your organization.

2.   Understand what you want to accomplish.

3.   Seek support before acting.

4.   Connect with individuals on your subject (head and heart).

5.   Understand your environment (politics).

6.   Make sure people take action.

Influence Exercise #1
In the space below, document your answers to the following questions:
Consider being in a heated discussion with your colleague. How would you influence your and his/her emotions in order to have your colleague see the benefit of your point of view?
1.
2.
3.
4.
5.

Influence Exercise #2

Select a topic you are passionate about. Write a convincing 3-paragraph essay to demonstrate that your opinion is the correct one. Document how you would organize your thoughts and provide a compelling argument to influence the reader's decision.

Influence Exercise #3

Repeat the above exercise and select a topic that you are less passionate about. Write a convincing 3-paragraph essay to demonstrate that your opinion is the correct one. Document how you would organize your thoughts and provide a compelling argument to influence the reader's decision.

Influence Exercise #4

Point/Counterpoint

Pick a word or a situation. Take one (1) minute and document all the pros for this stance. After one (1) minute, switch to the opposing position (opposite point of view). Share your work with someone to get his or her perception of how influential you were from each perspective.

Topic: _____

Point

1.

2.

3.

4.

5.

6.

7.

8.

9.

10.

Counter Point

1.

2.

3.

4.

5.

6.

7.

8.

9.

10.

Practice what you have learned from these exercises as often as you can to help build your core ability to influence.

CHAPTER 7

Critical Thinking Skills

Critical thinking is the ability to see the big picture and question how you got there!

Dr. Amanda Goodson

7. Critical Thinking Skills

What are Critical Thinking Skills?

    Critical thinking skills include the ability to see the big picture, pull back to the present, and then analyze what is needed to reach a desired result in a timely manner.

    Critical thinking skills are the ability to evaluate the relevant information to drive to an appropriate solution.

Why are critical thinking skills so important?

    Leaders should have the ability to think critically to assess all parts of a problem in order to identify an effective solution.

    The leader should be able to look at each piece of data and then determine how it fits into the final solution in order to make the organization effective.

How do I understand how to think critically?

1. Identify your thinking style:
    a. Analytical: clear thinking, orderly and rational
    b. Inquisitive: curious, alert and interested in the surrounding world
    c. Insightful: prudent, humble, reflective and strategic
    d. Open-minded: intellectually tolerant and fair-minded
    e. Systematic: conceptual, process-oriented and intuitive
    f. Timely: efficient, reliable, and responsive
    g. Truth-seeking: independent, tough-minded and skeptical
       (Note: No one style is better than the other, and we often use a balance that results in a better decision-making ability) Source:
       http://www.thinkwatson.com/mythinkingstyles

2. Identity the problem that you have to resolve.

3. Identify the solution you are seeking to achieve in your organization or on your team.

4. Using data or qualitative analysis for each step, list the pieces that need to come together to resolve the problem.

Critical Thinking Skills Exercise #1

Write your answers to the following questions in the space below:

Brainstorm the problems you are having within your organization:

1.
2.
3.
4.
5.

What is the end result you hope to achieve?

1.
2.
3.
4.
5.

If you were to translate your problem into several pieces, what would they be?

1.
2.
3.
4.
5.

Critical Thinking Skills Exercise #2

Write your answers to the following questions in the space below:

Develop a survey with your problem pieces (from the previous exercise), and ask others for potential solutions to your problem. Document your findings in the space below:

Take each piece of your problem listed in the previous exercise and develop a solution action plan based upon your survey feedback:

1.
2.
3.
4.
5.

Critical Thinking Skills Exercise #3

Assess your big picture solution and identify missing gaps in the space below:

1.
2.
3.
4.
5.

Develop a revised plan of action based on your gap assessment and the survey results in the space below:

Critical Thinking Skills Exercise #4

Develop a follow-up plan with stakeholders to see how effective your implementation plan is in meeting the organizations objectives.

CHAPTER 8

Excellence

Excellence is being the best in a place where you are needed and noticed. Stay in that place, and knock it out of the park!

Dr. Amanda Goodson

8. Excellence

What is Leadership Excellence?

> Leadership excellence is doing your very best and using your best resources to be the best you can be.

Why is leadership excellence important?

> Excellence in leadership is important because through excellence you will give your very best products and services to your organization and team. It is also important because you will experience sustained wins and grow your business potential through your best efforts.

How do I understand how to become an excellent leader?

1. Identify your place of greatest potential.

2. Identify a place where you are passionate for your work.

3. Identify area where the organization needs to improve, grow or emerge.

4. Place yourself in positions of opportunity where you are able to use your greatest potential, skill and passion in a place of great need for the organization.

5. Develop an excellence plan using your best skills for the organization.

Leadership Excellence Exercise #1
In the space below, write your answers to the following questions:
Brainstorm what you are passionate about:
1.
2.
3.
4.
5.

How does this area of passion help to improve and move toward the organization's vision/goals/objectives?
1.
2.
3.
4.
5.

What do you bring to the table that is excellent and that the organization needs?

1.
2.
3.
4.
5.

What do you bring to the table that is excellent, that the organization has not noticed about you?

1.
2.
3.
4.
5.

How can you get the organization to see your areas of strength and the areas that they have not tapped into?

1.
2.
3.
4.
5.

Leadership Excellence Exercise #2

In the space below, write your answers to the following questions:
Leadership excellence includes the ability to inspire others to excellence. Think about the ways you can motivate people in your organization to excellence.

1.
2.
3.
4.
5.

What are the places of opportunity where you are able to use your greatest potential, skill and passion in a place of great need for the organization?

1.
2.
3.
4.
5.

List ways to demonstrate genuine interest in the future path of your team members' careers.
1.
2.
3.
4.
5.

Leadership Excellence Exercise #3

In the space below, write your answers to the following questions:

Giving effective feedback to your team, both positive and negative, is essential to excellence in leadership. List the times when positive feedback may be beneficial for your organization?
1.
2.
3.
4.
5.

Consider the times when negative feedback may be used to spur your organization to make necessary changes or improvements.
1.
2.
3.
4.
5.

CHAPTER 9

Ambassadorship

Ambassadors represent the organization in a way that speaks well of the organization. They are the voice of the organization.

Dr. Amanda Goodson

9. Ambassadorship

What is Ambassadorship in leadership?

Ambassadorship in leadership is the unique ability to represent your organization without a personal agenda or hidden motive. Ambassadorship is a way of thinking which includes you being all in, and totally committed, with no reservations.

Note: Integrity and ethical leadership is required in Ambassadorship.

Why is this important?

This is important because the person charged with the assignment should behave in a trustworthy manner to complete their assignments and effectively influence others around them.

How do I understand how to become an ambassador as a leader?

1.   Recognize the way you see yourself and how you impact and influence the organization through your contributions to the organization.

2. Identity being all in. Be willing to be completely dedicated to your organizational vision and goals.

3. We willing to lead and advocate for the organizational vision and goals.

4. Envision yourself as an ambassador on an important assignment that can only be fulfilled by you.

5. Identify what steps are needed to be a better ambassador in your organization.

Ambassador Exercise #1
In the space provided below, list the answers to the following questions:
List the current vision of your organization:

_____
_____
_____

What does your organization value:

_____
_____
_____

What are your personal core values?

_____

_____

_____

Ambassador Exercise #2

In what ways do your personal values fit into your organization's values?

1.
2.
3.
4.
5.

List the ways you can be more dedicated to the vision, values and goals/objectives of your organization?

1.
2.
3.
4.
5.

Ambassador Exercise #3

Write a personal ambassador statement in alignment with your organization's vision, values and goals/objectives in the space below:

CHAPTER 10

Relationship

Life is about relationships

F.E. Cross

10. Relationships

What is Leadership Relationship?
> Leadership relationships allow people to be and celebrate themselves. Be you; be authentic.

Why is it important?
> A successful life is based on successful relationships.

How do I understand how to become a relationship leader?

1. Establishing a successful relationship is about listening. When engaged in a dialogue one needs to truly listen. Often times this requires turning the mind off from the perspective of trying to form an answer to respond; but listening to understand.

2. Trust is essential in a good leader/follower relationship.

3. Be approachable.

4. Be willing to work with others to collaborate on a solution to an issue.

Leadership Relationship Exercise #1
In the space below, document the answers to the following questions.
Think back to when you had many successful relationships. List the top 5:
1.
2.
3.
4.
5.

Document what you believe made these relationships successful:
1.
2.
3.
4.
5.

Leadership Relationship Exercise #2

Document the people with whom you want to have successful relationships. (*Note: this could be 1 person, or 100 people. It's up to you.*)

1.
2.
3.
4.
5.

Define the benefit you and that individual would receive if you have a successful relationship with them. (*Note: This has to be done for each person with whom you want to have a successful relationship.*)

1.
2.
3.
4.
5.

Determine and document what you are willing to do to have a successful relationship with this person. (*Note: This has to be done for each person with whom you want to have a successful relationship.*)

1.
2.
3.
4.
5.

Determine and document what you are NOT willing to do to have a successful relationship with this person (i.e. the boundaries of what you are not willing to put up with). (*Note: This has to be done for each person with whom you want to have a successful relationship.*)

1.
2.
3.
4.
5.

Congratulations you now have a clear picture of the following:

Who you want to have a successful relationship with.

The benefit you believe each of you will receive from this relationship.

What you are willing to do to achieve this successful relationship.

What you are not willing to do to have this successful relationship. (i.e., the boundaries of what you are not willing to put up with.)

Go out - champion and be the relationship leader that you are designed to be.

CHAPTER 11

Sowing and Reaping

A seed will produce after its kind. What you sow, you will reap!

Dr. Amanda Goodson

11. Sowing and Reaping

What is Sowing and Reaping as a leader?

Sowing is putting quality time into others in the workplace. It is making an investment into others. Reaping is the benefit of seeing how your time benefited others. It is seeing the success of an individual, organization or group that was directly impacted by your efforts.

Why is this important?

Sowing and reaping is important because your efforts will cause professional growth in others and increased productivity and/or a more cohesive group within your organization.

Sowing and reaping is important because it is the seed and catalyst to cause others to be successful.

Sowing and reaping is a selfless activity that takes one beyond his or her self to a place of assisting and helping others.

How do I understand how to sow and reap?

1. Sowing and reaping is seen as your contribution to the organization through coaching and/or mentoring others.

2. Sowing and reaping shows how you lead with authority, invest time and attention to others in the organization, and get a tangible return on your investment.

3. Sowing and reaping takes your best strengths and applies them to help others become stronger, and it yields a better return on your investment.

4. Sowing and reaping is taking your lessons learned and helping another person shorten the learning curve by using the skills and techniques to make their work products better, faster and more mature.

Sowing and Reaping Exercise #1

Document the answers to the following questions in the space below.

Make a list of people, processes or areas that can benefit from your expertise:

1.
2.
3.
4.
5.

From your list, give details of how your expertise can help them:

1.
2.
3.
4.
5.

Sowing and Reaping Exercise #2

From your list give details of when you will choose to help make things better. *(Note: for people, set up a time to mentor/coach them; if they are willing. For processes, develop a revised process, document it, and present it to your boss. For other areas, be specific.)*

1.
2.
3.
4.
5.

Sowing and Reaping Exercise #3

In the space below, make a list of how you will reward your accomplishments in helping others to succeed. *(Note: you may want to treat yourself to the movies, write yourself a thank you note, etc. - be creative)*

1.
2.
3.
4.
5.

Conclusion

We trust that by documenting and implementing the key principles in this workbook, you will begin to see remarkable improvements in your relationships and in your performance at all levels. You will also be able to allow them to make things happen around you.

As stated in our *How to Unlock Your Full Potential* mini-book, those who act on what they know will develop the skills needed to reach peak states in the organizations they influence. I believe we have all been granted the ability to accomplish great things. Greatness has many facets and levels. Greatness carries power; and the power to carry out our tasks can be done well with the right desire.

The information in this workbook is to serve to equip you with the documented tools that will provide valuable insights into how to lead with power and influence. People who unlock their full potential have the ability to lead more effectively, transform themselves and others around them, be authentic, achieve, grow professionally, influence others in amazing ways, think more critically and solve hard problems, walk in excellence, be a global thinker and ambassador, have lasting relationships, and produce great results.

This workbook was meant to stir up your thinking and cause you to be more creative, enhance your leadership knowledge, and develop a style that will impact others around you with power. Continue to keep an open mind so that you will be able to see how walking in the authority of a leader will continue to affect you. This will enable you to learn new skills to transform your thinking and touch those whose lives you influence.

Thank you for reading our book and completing our workbook. Enjoy your journey as you continue to unlock your full potential and live an awesome life!!

I look forward to seeing you in the next leadership mini-book and workbook!!

BIBLIOGRAPHY

Business Dictionary. *Business Dictionary.com* (Achievement Oriented Leadership: Definition). Retrieved November, 2013, from www.businessdictionary.com/definition/leadership.htm.

Goodson, Dr. Amanda. (2012). *Authority of a Leader*. Tucson: Amanda Goodson Publishing.

Goodson, Dr. Amanda. (2012). *Powerful People Lead*. Tucson: Amanda Goodson Publishing.

Goodson, Dr. Amanda. (2012). *Seed Planting Harvest Expecting*. Tucson: Amanda Goodson Publishing.

Think Watson. *ThinkWatson.com* (Thinking Styles). Retrieved November, 2013, from www.thinkwatson.com/mythinkingstyles.

Wikipedia. *Wikipedia.com* (Achievement: Definition). Retrieved November, 2013, from http://en.wikipedia.org/wiki/Achievement.

About the Authors:

Frederick Cross

Fred is an author, public/motivational speaker and has held positions of increasing responsibilities for the U.S. Department of Defense and for Fortune 100 companies. These positions have included Business Area Growth Manager, Program Manager, Logistic Manager, Strategic/Mobilization Planner, and Production Controller/Production Engineer. He holds a Bachelor's of Science in Industrial Technology and a Master of Business Administration.

Dr. Amanda H. Goodson

Amanda is an author, educator, facilitator, inspirational speaker and coach for corporations, agencies and non-profit organizations. Amanda inspires others and connects with her audiences by sharing real-life experiences using enthusiastic, energizing, and interactive methods. Amanda has a Bachelor's of Science in Electrical Engineering, a Master's of Science in Management, and a Doctor of Ministry Church Administration.

Odetta S. Scott

Odetta is an author and engineer who is passionate about people development, continuous improvement, and organizational effectiveness. Odetta's charismatic authenticity and transparency allows her to connect with her audiences and inspire them to want to learn and improve. Odetta has a Bachelor's of Science in Mechanical Engineering Technology, a Master of Business Administration, and a Master's of Science in Organizational Development.

To contact Fred Cross:
fecross85@yahoo.com

To contact Dr. Amanda Goodson:
www.AmandaGoodson.com

To contact Odetta Scott:
osscott22@yahoo.com